...far above rubies

Deidra Saddler

Copyright © 2016 by Deidra Saddler

All rights reserved. No part of this publication may be reproduced, stored in a retrieval system, or transmitted by any means without prior permission in writing from the author.

Unless otherwise noted, all Scripture quotations are from the New King James Version of the Bible Copyright 1982 by Thomas Nelson, Inc. Used by permission. All rights reserved. http://www.nelsonbibles.com/

Scripture quotations marked "AMP" are taken from the Amplified Bible, Copyright 1954, 1958, 1962, 1964, 1965, 1987 by The Lockman Foundation. Used by permission. www.Lockman.org

Scripture quotations marked (NIV) are taken from the Holy Bible, New International Version, NIV.

Copyright 1973, 1978, 1984 by Biblica, Inc.

Used by permission of Zondervan. All rights reserved worldwide. http://www.zondervan.com

Scripture quotations marked "MSG" or "The Message" are taken from The Message. Copyright 1993, 1994, 1995, 1996, 2000, 2001, 2002. Used by permission of NavPress Publishing Group. http://www.navpress.com/

Published in United States of America by Faith Walk Publishing LLC

Learn more information at: www.faithwalkpublishing.com

ISBN: 978-0-9905163-5-4

First Edition: JUNE 2016

10 9 8 7 6 5 4 3 2 1

Table of Contents

INTRODUCTION..V

CHAPTER ONE: DESCENT INTO DEPRECIATION 1

CHAPTER TWO: GOD CARES FOR YOU 19

CHAPTER THREE: DARKNESS BEFORE DAWN................. 35

CHAPTER FOUR: ASSURANCE POLICY 69

CHAPTER FIVE: RECOVERY OF WORTH 75

Introduction

God said, *"Daughter your value is FAR ABOVE RUBIES OR PEARLS."*

It sadly took me a journey of 20 years that consisted of repairing my self-worth and re-building my self-esteem to believe this, and to finally allow it to be firmly implanted in my heart.

It is my sincerest desire that this book will help make your journey length a fraction of that, by allowing you to look into my dark heart moments so that your dark heart moments can be revealed and healed.

A capable, intelligent, and virtuous woman—who is he who can find her? She is far more precious than jewels and her value is far above rubies or pearls. (AMP)

CHAPTER ONE

Descent into Depreciation

"For we are glad when we are weak ([a] unapproved) and you are really strong. And this we also pray for: your all-round strengthening and perfecting of soul." 2 Corinthians 13:9 (AMP)

In the middle of 2015, my pastor preached a sermon about value. I often take notes during the sermons; sometimes they are direct quotes, sometimes they are inspired thoughts received during the message, and at other times they are questions asked of me by the Lord. During this particular time of teaching, my notes were a barrage of questions. One question in particular had me puzzled and I pondered it the entire week. The Father had asked me,

"Why don't you ask Me for things?"

Now of course I refuted this question with, But Lord I ask you for things all the time? To which He responded,

"For others. Why don't you ask Me for you?"

I knew this was going to be a learning experience, and in order for the answer to be found, I undoubtedly was going to take a journey through some painful time in my past that I had not consciously registered as significant. So I braced myself for the ride.

I have come into an understanding about the way Holy Spirit deals with me. Whenever there is something to be learned, The Father asks me a question, and in response, I have to ask the question that will kick-start the lesson. My question became, *"Father why don't I ask you for things for me?"*

This was the doorway to the root of the issue. Just in case you are not sure what the issue is exactly, the issue is trust.

Now you may say *"I thought this was a chapter on value or the lack of it, where did this lack of trust come from?"* I promise you, I am not floundering all over the place. This is a chapter on value; but if you are familiar with the ways of God when He is restoring one back to wholeness, He deals with the root of a situation, and in my case (and often others), the root of why I didn't ask Him for things for me was directly tied to my lack of trust. It wasn't in His capability that I had no trust, but in my value as a daughter that had the privilege of being able to ask.

What does that mean? It means I felt depreciated. Now, coming into this revelation required a stroll down childhood lane. Before I take you with me, I want to say that this is not a bashing of my parents. I have come to understand that parents can only give their children what they themselves have. This is why training them up in a relationship with The Father is so key, because He can fill in the gaps and holes that are present to cause detriment.

The Bible says in the 22nd chapter of Proverbs, *"Train up a child in the way he should go; and when he is old, he will not depart from it."*

Previously I stated that I felt depreciated as a daughter. The definition of **depreciate** is, ***"to diminish in value over a period of time."*** Holy Spirit began with a memory of returned jewelry to show me that my descent into depreciation as a daughter started when I was just thirteen years of age.

I was what my elementary school called a *"Gifted"* student. This allowed me to skip a grade, and so I graduated from elementary school three months after my thirteenth birthday. My father bought me a beautiful gold necklace as a graduation gift. The chain was thin with my birthstone in the center of a gold pendant heart. I loved that necklace, my skin however did not. After my neck turned a shade darker than the rest of my body and I broke out in a rash, my father took me and the necklace back to the jeweler he had purchased it from. I stood by as my father angrily accused the jeweler of cheating him and selling him inferior merchandise. My father screamed,

"This was a present for my little girl's graduation and it is NOT 14 karat gold like you said it was!"

He then proceeded to pull me forward as he pointed to my neck.

"LOOK AT HER NECK! IT'S BLACK AND ALL BROKEN OUT!" "IF THIS WAS 14 KARAT GOLD HER NECK WOULD NOT LOOK LIKE THIS!"

The man nervously looked at my neck and then requested to see the necklace that my father held clenched in his hand. He took it and went directly to the little gold tag near the clasp.

"Sir, I am sorry about your daughter's neck, but this necklace is 14 karats. See here, the tag states it as so. I did not cheat you, sir."

My father quickly responded with,

"Then WHY does her neck look like THAT?"

The man cautiously replied,

"Sir, your daughter seems to have very sensitive skin and requires a higher, more expensive karat of gold."

My father looked at me and stated,

"Then her husband is going to have to buy it for her, because I ain't."

He returned the necklace, got his money back, and we left the store. My worth had lost some of its value, but I didn't know it then. The Holy Spirit continued to take me on my revelation tour with a second memory.

The following year in the fall while collecting my sophomore class schedule, my friends were all excited. You see, Driver's Education was a part of the sophomore curriculum, and when asked by friends the day and time I would be in class, I found that it had been removed from my schedule. I brought this miscarriage of justice to my father, who promptly took me the next day into the counselor's office to find out why? The counselor told my father that although I was a sophomore, I was not technically eligible to take the course.

"Your daughter is only 14, Mr. Saddler. The legal age for a student to learn to drive in Illinois is 16. It seems that her brilliance is going to hold her back from participating until she is a senior – of which at that time, you will have to pay for the course."

My father was fine with the beginning of the counselor's statement but he took offense to the ending of it.

"Wait a minute here, you mean to tell me that my daughter is being penalized for being smart? And did you say pay? That I will have to pay for her to take the course in 2 years? Why? There is no cost for her to take the course now, why would I have to pay for her to take it then?"

The counselor responded with,

"We are not penalizing your daughter for being intelligent sir. The course is a required free

course within sophomore curriculum; however, it is considered a makeup course for seniors. All make-up courses require payment from the family because they are summer school courses. Your daughter will not be eligible to take driver's education until she has turned 16, which in her case will be when she is a senior, and unfortunately is only offered as a summer school course. I apologize but it is really out of our control."

My father looked at me and then back to the counselor and replied,

"Then she will learn to drive when she is grown and on her own. I am not going to pay for something for her that is free for everyone else!"

Right there at that moment, my worth as a daughter depreciated again, this time to half of its potential. (I did not learn to drive until I was 26 years old under the instruction of a man whom I was in a relationship with) The tour was not yet complete. I had one more memory to return to.

The rest of my value diminished when I turned 15 and my father had remarried. I had gotten in a physical altercation with his new wife and she gave him an ultimatum,

"Either she goes or I go. The both of us can NOT live here!"

My father turned to me and asked,

"Where do you want to live? With your mother or my sister?"

At that moment he died to me, which caused me to battle for the next ten years with un-forgiveness and rejection. But not only that, the rest of my already unstable self-worth was depleted, and I, unbeknownst to me had wholeheartedly embraced the lie that the enemy over time had patiently sculpted with the shattered pieces of my value. The lie being that I, as a daughter, was not worth the effort.

Who but God and the enemy of course knew that returning a necklace, refusing to pay for a Driver's Education Course, and removing me from my childhood home would result in the deeply-rooted belief of diminished value? I no longer trusted that I had the right as a daughter to ask my father for anything. I had no problem asking from my sisters, but I didn't ask my father for anything for myself until I was almost 40 years old – and even then, it was for the sake of my daughter that I had asked at that time.

The connection between how I viewed my biological father is greatly intertwined with how I viewed my heavenly one. You see, because I did not believe in my value as a daughter within my relationship with my earthly father, this was a direct cause of why I **wouldn't** ask God the Heavenly Father for things I needed or wanted.

My soul had a want. It desperately wanted to know that I was worth the extra effort. The desire it sought would have been satisfied had my father bought the more expensive necklace, and had been willing to pay for the driver's education class in my senior year. My soul also had a need. I needed to be seen as an equal priority in my father's heart. Had I been allowed to stay in my childhood home with my siblings after the ultimatum was given to him, my value would have been anchored. But instead, I began slowly over time to believe that as a daughter, I wasn't worth much.

Some time ago during a conversation with my maternal grandmother, I learned that I wasn't a planned pregnancy for my mom. And much later, after a conversation with my paternal grandmother, I was informed that because my mother was pregnant with me, my father felt obligated to marry her to keep her from becoming homeless. Combine this information with the earlier incidents and you have the perfect recipe for devaluation. The enemy added to what had happened in my youth, physically, verbally, and emotionally abusive relationships for good measure; and low self-worth was allowed to become firmly rooted. My identity as a daughter had taken a severe blow.

Years later, salvation comes, and I am taught,

"But to as many as did receive and welcome Him, He gave the authority (power, privilege, right) to become the children of God, that is, to those who believe in (adhere to, trust in, and rely on) His name," John 1:12 (AMP)

and,

"For He foreordained us (destined us, planned in love for us) to be adopted (revealed) as His own children through Jesus Christ, in accordance with the purpose of His will [[a]because it pleased Him and was His kind intent]— Ephesians 1:5 (AMP)

The message revealed within these scriptures is that I was not only saved from damnation, but I was also adopted, and God was now my Father. If He is now my father, then by natural deduction I am His *daughter*.

According to the first scripture, I have privileges and rights as this new *daughter t*o trust in God as a child does a father to provide, protect, and guide me. The problem was that I had not been able to do that in my natural life; and so I erroneously assumed that just as my natural father had unknowingly programmed me **not** to see the value in being one of his daughters, this new *father/daughter* relationship was going to be the exact same.

Many sermons have been taught from the 22nd chapter of Proverbs, which instructs parents to teach their children to walk in the guiding of the LORD. But what I think we miss and do not highlight within these teachings is that if you train that child in the wrong ways and thoughts, when they get old, they will not depart from those either, at least not without a lot of pain and suffering mixed in. The Message Bible says it this way,

> *"Point your kids in the right direction—when they're old they won't be lost."*

Because I was not pointed in the right direction, accepting God as my SAVIOR was to a degree somewhat easy; but accepting HIM as my *Father*, now that was going to take some doing. This pause caused the beginning and the middle phases of my adulthood and Christian walk to be lived as an extremely lost individual.

Why? Well, because I made an unconscious decision not to ask God for anything that resembled a need or a want. I may have been adopted, but I didn't receive the rights and privileges that come with said adoption. Pay close attention to my words here. I didn't say that God *didn't give* me the rights and privileges that come with His adoption; I said that I <u>*didn't receive*</u> them, because they came with stipulations.

The stipulations are: those that trust in and rely on His name, those He gave authority, power, privilege, and the right to become. In my unconscious decision not to ask, I in turn was deciding not to **trust in** or **rely on** Him – and without these two *must do's,* I have no access to the rights and privileges that He has given with the adoption.

In 2 Corinthians 6:18 the LORD says, *"And I will be a Father to you, and you shall be My sons and daughters, says the Lord Almighty."*

Most people who read or hear these words feel great joy, but in me was great dread. In my mind God the Father was one more father that I wouldn't matter to.

This erroneous belief was buried at the root of my trust issue. I was not conscious of it. In all sincerity, I truly thought that I had accepted everything that came with the gift of salvation, but I hadn't. And because I hadn't, my needs and desires were something that I had to get on my own, and so my relationship with the Lord was guarded to say the least.

"Restore to me the joy of Your salvation and uphold me with a willing spirit." Ps.51:12 (AMP)

DAUGHTER SELF-EXAMINATION

1. As you read the chapter, what has the Holy Spirit revealed to you about how you view your own value as one of GOD'S daughters?

___

2. What lies do you now see that you have accepted as truth about your worth?

___

3. Daughters, as you read this chapter, has the Holy Spirit revealed a need for you to forgive your father? If so, pray now the following:

Father God I now see where the loss of my value as a daughter first began to unravel, in the name of Jesus I ask you to help me to forgive my father for_____. Father as you begin to realign my worth with your plumb line, I renounce the lies of the enemy that had me believing that You did not care for me and that I had not the privilege to ask You in faith for the things that pertaineth to life. Your Word says that if I delight myself also in You oh Lord, that You shall give me the desires of my heart. The desire of my heart today is to be free from the bondages of low self-esteem, and to know without doubt and total faith that I can trust in our relationship as Father and daughter. I desire to have total restoration of the love, care and respect that an earthly father and a daughter should share between them, or to at least be able to do as Your Word says to make every effort to live in peace with everyone and to be holy. In Jesus Name. Amen.

FATHER SELF-EXAMINATION

4. Fathers have you shown your daughter(s) the value in being your child? If no, why not?

_____

5. Do you see any areas within your affirmation of your daughter(s) that may have doorways for the enemy to come in and pervert their self- image?

_____

6. Fathers, if while you were reading this book the Holy Spirit began to reveal incidents that are potential worth-destroying moments, go now and rectify the situation. As long as there is breath, it is never too late as you prepare to go pray the prayer below.

Lord Jesus forgive me where I have lacked in my responsibility as a father toward the daughter(s) you have blessed me with. Show me how to reverse the damage that I unknowingly have caused my daughter's self-worth. Guide my tongue to speak life-affirming words that will break the strongholds of the enemy in the areas of self-esteem that I opened for havoc to be wreaked. Repair the breaches and fortify our relationship stronger than it was before. Return me unto my rightful position in her life and heart. Thank you for opening my eyes to those things that I was unaware of that could have derailed her walk with You. I trust You LORD GOD to move in this situation to correct every crooked way. As I commit myself to be led by Your Holy Spirit to become the steadfast example in her life, help me to allow YOU to be seen in my words, actions and expressions of love in Jesus Name. Amen.

CHAPTER TWO

God Cares for You

"Casting the [a]whole of your care [all your anxieties, all your worries, all your concerns, [b] once and for all] on Him, for He cares for you affectionately and cares about you [c]watchfully."
1 Peter 5:7 (Amp)

God is gracious and did not leave me in a guarded view of Him. He began to show me in little ways that I did not have to depend upon myself alone. Once when getting ready to go grocery shopping, my usual routine was interrupted. I had four small children to care for and I didn't have a vehicle. While they were in school I would catch the bus to the store and then a cab home with my groceries. However, on this day, the Holy Spirit sent a church member to my apartment just when I was leaving. She asked where I was on my way to and I told her the grocery store. She then asked how was I going to get there, and I replied by bus. This prompted her to ask how I was going to get my groceries home. I told her, that I would take a cab home. She stood there with a look of unbelief on her face.

When I asked what was wrong, her reply shocked me.

"You will allow pride to stop you from getting the help that you need?"

I of course didn't understand this response. **Pride?** How was my monthly trip to the grocery store connected in any way to pride? She went on to explain.

"Deidra you have four children, and you are working a minimum wage job. You are willing to spend extra money that I am pretty sure you do not have on bus and cab fare to grocery shop instead of asking one of us with a car to take you?"

My fail safe responses were always,

"I don't want to impose. It's fine really I've gotten used to it, it really isn't that bad."

But I did mind, and it was that bad. She looked at me and said, **"God cares about you. Get in the car."** From that moment on, she made it her business to come by every month around the same time to make sure that I was not taking a bus and a cab to get groceries. This she did until I was able to get a car of my own.

"What is man that You are mindful of him, And the son of man that You visit him?" Ps.8:4(NKJV)

"God cares about you." That statement rang in my ears for months, years even. The Father wanted me to see that even something as mundane as getting groceries is on His radar. Groceries are a necessity, transportation is a necessity, and I needed to understand that God as my Father cares about my needs. Not just my need for eternal salvation but every need that pertains to life on this side of heaven both big and small. Is this something that you need to see as well?

"The Lord is my shepherd; I shall not want." Ps.23:1(KJV)

God cares about you as a daughter even when you make decisions without Him that are not the decisions He had within His plan for your life. How do I know?

Well, in 1995 I made a decision to move to Iowa. I had gone there to visit the man I would later marry and ultimately divorce. During visits with him, I would research employment and housing; and on my last visit there, I secured three houses to choose from – or so I thought.

When the time came, my friends helped me pack up my 24-feet U-haul truck. I took the keys to my soon-to-be sister-in-law, so that she and her husband could drive my things to their hometown later in the week for me. In the car, I packed up my four children and snacks for the road and set out for my new life. I arrived in Waterloo around 3pm that afternoon, and headed to my new soon-to-be grandmother-in-law's home.

After unloading the children, I went into town to meet the leasing agent that I had been working with a month prior and had left my good faith deposit with. To my surprise, the office was no longer there. It took a minute for me to grasp the fact that my deposit was gone, right along with the three choices of housing. The ride back to grandma's was the longest ride of trepidation that I had ever taken. I dreaded with every fiber of my being walking into her home to inform her that I had been conned, and that housing along with some of my money was gone. As grace would have it, I didn't have to; because when I walked in, the look on my face told the whole story. She took one look at me and asked only one question,

"Baby what are you going to do?"

I had no idea. I was in a new city with four children. I did not really know anyone except his family, and those acquaintances were short. I didn't know the area all that well, and there was a truck on its way in 24 hours loaded with all of my things; I had absolutely nowhere for my family or my things to go. (*Do you see all the I's*) At that moment I decided that I needed some alone time with the Lord, but in grandma's house there wasn't a room (*including the bathroom*) that wasn't occupied by a person. The need to be alone with GOD grew steadily. I hadn't prayed about making this move before I made it, but I was in trouble and I surely was about to pray now!

"God is our refuge and strength, a very present help in trouble." Ps.46:1(KJV)

To the backyard I went. Straight to my car, and there I sat with the windows rolled up and began to pray. I said,

"Ok God, You have been trying to show me for months now that You care about me. I know that I should have prayed and asked you for Your advice on this move before I made it. For that I am sorry. I ask You to forgive me."

The next part of this prayer was a bit harder for me to say.

"Lord.... I .... need ...I need your help. I have brought my children here believing that I had three choices of housing, my furniture will be on its way here in a few hours and I don't have anywhere to put it. I really don't want to ask grandma to move in. I don't know her all that well. Please help me find a place to stay I have less than 24 hours. In Jesus name I pray. Amen."

"If God gives such attention to the appearance of wildflowers—most of which are never even seen—don't you think he'll attend to you, take pride in you, do his best for you? What I'm trying to do here is to get you to relax, to not be so preoccupied with getting, so you can respond to God's giving. People who don't know God and the way he works fuss over these things, but you know both God and how he works. Steep your life in God-reality, God-initiative, God-provisions. Don't worry about missing out. You'll find all your everyday human concerns will be met." Matthew 6:30-33 (Message)

After I was done praying, and crying, and yes, begging, I wiped my face, straightened my hair, and went into the house. Grandma was sitting in the kitchen waiting for me to enter. I came in and sat down at the table across from her. She looked at me intently for a moment before beginning the following conversation;

"So you went and had a little talk with Jesus did you?"

"Yes ma'am."

"Well do you believe that he heard you?"

"Yes ma'am."

"Good. Down the block there on the corner is a friend of mine. He owns properties around town. He happens to be at the house there getting it ready to rent. Go down there and see if he has any available properties. Tell him I sent you."

I sat there dazed.

"Go on now. For him, time is money. He's down there at the corner house – and remember, tell him I sent you."

I came back with an 8am appointment to see one of his properties that was about five blocks away from grandma. When I returned to grandma's the next morning after the appointment, I came back with the keys to my new rental, a three-bedroom house. Thirty minutes later, my sister-in-law pulled up to her grandma's house with my furniture, a week after that I became employed.

God was officially being moved into the "Daddy" slot in my mind, but my heart still needed some convincing. You may be shocked that I said that, so let me explain the statement. My pastor has a saying that he is fond of repeating, *"We say that we give God our whole heart; but in actuality, we give Him the parts that are not blocked."* My heart still had not at that time been exposed to the deeply-rooted truth that I explained in chapter one. Remember, that revelation was just given this year in 2015, this incident happened 20 years earlier.

It is totally possible to have head knowledge of The Father and not have Him in your heart. Now, it is quite an unfortunate state of being, but a totally possible state nevertheless.

> *"Therefore the Lord said: "Inasmuch as these people draw near with their mouths and honor*

Me with their lips, but have removed their hearts far from Me, And their fear toward Me is taught by the commandment of men," Isa. 29:13 (KJV)

<u>*"And their fear toward Me is taught by the commandment of men."*</u> I would like to further explain the statement about my heart still needing convincing with the use of the above verse. Yes, I had confessed Jesus as my Lord and Savior. Yes, I believed that Jesus died and rose for my sins. Yes, I was a faithful tithe-giving worshipper of Christ. Yes, I went to Sunday School, BTU, Vacation Bible School, mid-week Bible Study. I became a Pastor's Aide, Sunday School Teacher, and choir member. And despite all that, my heart was not totally given to God.

Everything I did and participated in was done because I was <u>*taught*</u> that this is what you do once you become a Christian. (those commandments of men) Not once was there prayer to God to ask Him where He wanted me to serve in His Kingdom. My Christian activity was predicated on the by-laws of the Baptist Training Union, and The Apostle's Creed that had belief number nine tweaked a bit to exclude the Catholic Church statement that became memorized and recited because tradition says so. (again those commandments of men)

The commandments of some men say women can't preach, that tongues are not for today, and that boards (deacon, trustee, mother) have the right to dictate what the Pastor preaches to the congregation. And this is how you can believe in Jesus, do all that I had done in the beginning and middle phases of my Christian walk, and still not have given God your whole heart. In all of that business, I still did not trust in my value as a daughter of the Most High God. And I still believed that I and I alone was responsible for my life needs.

But The Father kept on pressing the message, _"God cares for you"_ more and more in my mind until it would eventually find a permanent home in my heart. My move from Iowa and back to Minnesota was this time guided by prayer; and while on a visit to my old church there, _I asked_ for help, in the form of a loan, in order to get a truck to get my things back and to place them in storage. The truck was rented and driven by my former pastor. My storage was paid for 30 days, and after a few conversations I was given the keys to a fellow church member's apartment to sublease. Through it all God, was showing me that He cares for me.

Many months later, on the day that I brought in my last installment paying off the loan given by the church, my former pastor confided in me that the trustee board had voted against the loan. Their reasons were that I was young and did not know what I wanted in life. And they had no faith that I was going to pay the loan back. He laughed as he stated that I was the only person that had actually paid the church back of all the loans that had been given out. When I left his office that day, I heard again...
<u>"God cares for you."</u>

"Let each of you look out not only for his own interests, but also for the interests of others."
Philippians 2:4 (NKJV)

A few months after that, my car broke down at work and I didn't have the money to tow it. After a few days, believing it abandoned, the city towed it and I did not know where. My pastor found out where my car had been sent, paid the storage fines, had the car towed to his home, bought the parts needed, fixed the car, and brought it to me; all while refusing to allow me to repay him. Why?

"A father of the fatherless, a defender of widows, Is God in His holy habitation." Ps.68:5 (NKJV)

Because God was using him as an example of fatherhood. He was chipping away at the wall of lies that I had enclosed myself in. Those lies that told me that as a daughter I wasn't worth much.

Remember earlier, I had said that the truck was rented and driven by my pastor? God had begun the demolition at the moment He allowed the pastor to go against the suggestions of the board and give me the money. In his office that day of my final payment, he told me that he took the loan out in his name and so became the debtor in my place.

"Contribute to the needs of God's people [sharing in the necessities of the saints]; pursue the practice of hospitality." Romans 12:13 (AMP)

He then cleared his schedule and drove the truck from Minneapolis to Waterloo with his oldest daughter and her husband, and my soon to be sister-in-law and her husband. He helped pack up the truck and drove it back to Minneapolis, where he helped to unload my things into storage and paid for them for a month.

God through my pastor wanted me to see how valuable I was as a _daughter_. The Father was restoring my self-esteem. From that moment on, me and my children became a part of the pastor's family. Every Sunday after service, it was at their home we had dinner. He even included us in their family vacations all expenses paid. My pastor became my surrogate father and I became a third daughter to him and his wife. Still to this day when I am introduced by either of them, I am introduced as daughter, and by their daughters, I am introduced as sister.

> *"This is how we've come to understand and experience love: Christ sacrificed his life for us. This is why we ought to live sacrificially for our fellow believers, and not just be out for ourselves. If you see some brother or sister in need and have the means to do something about it but turn a cold shoulder and do nothing, what happens to God's love? It disappears. And you made it disappear." 1John 3:16-17 (Message)*

The Father caused my pastor and his family to bring scripture to life; and in doing so, my life was changed. I had a need to see my value and to feel my worth. Their actions allowed God's love to remain constant in my life and helped me make it through some hard trials later; because I was able to look back and remember how God lovingly showed me in all of these examples how much He cares for me.

GOD CARES FOR YOU! Just like He cares for me, and He wants to show you just like He showed me, how much you are worth.

REFLECTIONS

Daughter, where in your life have others outside your family been used by God to fill a need?

___

Daughters, are you because of deep hurt and fear, forbidding yourself to ask and or receive the help you need that others can provide?

___

Fathers, are you being pressed upon by the Holy Spirit to become a surrogate to the fatherless?

___

Fathers, are you willing to do the extra that it may take for someone who is not blood-related?

___

CHAPTER THREE

Darkness before Dawn

*"Unto the upright there arises light in the darkness;
He is gracious, and full of compassion, and
righteous." Psalms 112:4 (NKJV)*

In March of 1996, I married the gentleman that I, in flesh, had moved to Iowa to be near. He, in an effort to keep our relationship going, had moved to Minneapolis that January. Because of the conviction of the Lord and my adamant refusal to continue to play house (co-habitation), he asked for my hand in marriage. You would think that this blessed event would become one of the stepping stones into the recovery of my worth; sadly, the enemy used it as an instrument for the further destruction of it.

*"Trust God from the bottom of your heart; don't
try to figure out everything on your own. Listen
for God's voice in everything you do, everywhere*

you go; he's the one who will keep you on track. Don't assume that you know it all." Prov.3:5 (Message)

The first problem with the union was that I did not **<u>trust God</u>** as the scripture above states to. I married him because; **(a)** I was proving something to an ex, and **(b)** Lust, I had taken as justification for my actions the scripture 1 Corinthians 7:9, *"It is better to marry than to burn."* Even though I trusted that we loved one another, I strongly believe that he felt pressured into asking me because I refused to continue to fornicate with him, not because he truly desired to be wed at that time.

But the most detrimental problem with the union came in May, just two months after I said 'I do', my husband went on a two-week binge. He disappeared and took all of the money that was in the bank account with him. He had a drug addiction that I had not been informed of, and that he was able to hide because of our distance and the short four months that I had lived in the same city as he did. (We did not cohabit while I lived in Iowa).

During this time, my mind wandered into every perceivable tragedy imaginable. Did he overdose in some abandoned building? Had someone robbed him and left him for dead? Prayer and communication with his twin sister is what kept me from losing my entire mind. The enemy however, took a section of it, by latching onto the gateway that had been dropped into my life with the following comments,

"Look at you, you couldn't even manage to keep your new husband satisfied enough to want to be around you."

"I told you nobody wanted you."

"This is your punishment for having sex before marriage."

"This is what you are worth- a drug addict for a husband."

"He chose drugs over you."

These tormenting words of the enemy were sent to crush my self-esteem. I only partly rose above them out of sheer determination. I was taught a wife stands by her husband no matter what. And so we were going to beat this thing no matter what!

A light at the end of the tunnel seemed to be shining

through. In July, my husband and I became employed at the same distribution company. In August, he was fired. A week after that, the apartment complex where I had added his name to the lease called us in the office and informed us that we had to move, that he was not accepted because of his past prison record.

In an effort to identify his triggers, he informed me that the stress of being both unemployed and having to move was causing the desire for drugs to be awakened. We needed a plan immediately. I reached out to family. My brother who lived in Chicago stated that he could get my husband a job and my sister opened up her doors for us to move in. In September of 1996, I packed up the U-haul again, this time Chicago-bound.

> *"And we know that all things work together for good to those who love God, to those who are the called according to His purpose." Romans 8:28 (NKJV)*

The next seven years would be the most abusive years that I had ever experienced in my life. Because of the physical, emotional, verbal, and financial abuse suffered, my value as a wife, worth as a woman, and confidence as a mother hit an all-time low. I began to believe that because of the wrong choices made in my life, this was my lot and I had no right to ask God for anything better.

> *"He saved us, not because of any works of righteousness that we had done, but because of His own pity and mercy, by [the] cleansing [bath] of the new birth (regeneration) and renewing of the Holy Spirit," Titus 3:5 (Amp)*

In my past I had been a fornicator, an adulteress, unforgiving, and a stubbornly hard-hearted individual. In my mind of course, it was time for the chickens to come home to roost. Even after accepting Christ as my Savior while singing in the choir, working as a Pastor's Aide, and teaching Sunday school in Minneapolis, I was also fornicating.

Before I had even stepped foot inside a church, I had an affair with a married man, fornicated with a dozen others, and had spoken in such a way that my mouth put sailors to shame. My children were not treated as the gifts they were, and were afraid of me. And now, because I was married, God was supposed to overlook all of that and miraculously fix this broken situation? I was not about to get my hopes up and ask Him to do that so I prayed other things instead.

What did I pray? I prayed for me to be a better wife; one that would not upset her husband, *(because I in error believed that I was causing him to hit me and to use drugs)*. I prayed for my husband to become the father, and me the mother that my children needed. I prayed for all these things, believing that I was underserving of any of them. Have you been there? Have you ever prayed for something and not really believed that you are worthy of receiving it?

"Come to Me, all you who labor and are heavy-laden and overburdened, and I will cause you to rest. [I will [a]ease and relieve and [b] refresh [c]your souls.]" Matthew 11:28 (Amp)

I desperately desired rest. My soul was crying out for ease, relief and refreshing. What I needed was a renewed mind, of which of course I thought I already had received. My move to Chicago was going to prove that renewing the mind is not a one-time event like I thought, but a continual process.

In Chicago, under the guidance of a new pastor, I was taught how to pray effectively. There were classes on spiritual gifts and how to operate within them, classes on what worship is and what worship isn't, and classes about spiritual warfare where I learned of the many ways that Satan and his demons operate within the lives of people.

Underneath the spiritual guidance of the men and women of my new house of worship, I learned more than I ever dreamed possible within the word of God; but I still had **not** accepted the truth about my value as <u>*a daughter*</u>.

*"Strip yourselves of your former nature [put off and discard your old unrenewed self] which characterized your previous manner of life and becomes corrupt through lusts and desires that spring from delusion; And be constantly **renewed in the spirit of your mind** [having a fresh mental and spiritual attitude]," Ephesians 4:22-23*
(Amp)

It seemed that the more knowledgeable I became, the angrier my husband became. Training helped me to understand that it was not his thinking alone that perceived that I was now *"judging"* him, but the unclean spirits that tormented him. So I prayed. I tried to pray with him, but that didn't last so I prayed for him, I prayed for God to take the taste of drugs out of my husband's mouth, and surprisingly he left. At first it was into rehab programs for 30 days here, 90 days there, 6 months at another one, and then he moved out all the way back to Waterloo where he stayed gone for 2 years. During that time, I continued to pray.

"...Oh, that You would bless me and enlarge my border, and that Your hand might be with me, and You would keep me from evil so it might not hurt me!..." 1Chron.4:10 (Amp)

God allowed me to gain employment, purchase a home and a car. My outward life was good again. I started to hear that familiar verse, <u>*"God cares for you."*</u> And then one day out of the blue, my husband called me stating that he was drug free, and after a few phone conversations he and I agreed that he should return home.

"However, when He, the Spirit of truth, has come, He will guide you into all truth; for He will not speak on His own authority, but whatever He hears He will speak; and He will tell you things to come." John 16:13 (NKJV)

I called a family meeting and informed my children that my husband was coming home. I said to them that he was drug free and that we were not going to have any more problems like before. They sat in silence. My youngest son was the one who spoke first with a simple question,

"When?"

"When what son?"

"When will he be coming back here?"

"We made arrangements for him to be here next month. He's working and wants to give his notice and make a little extra money to bring home."

They sat there silent. I told them that they didn't have to trust him right away, that they could watch his actions and that he would prove to them that he had changed. I said this in an attempt to convince myself more than them that we were finally going to be a real family. Each one got up and left the living room; all except my oldest son, he sat there on the couch as if he was contemplating his next move. I decided not to question him and left him to his thoughts. How I wish I had.

Slowly, my oldest son's attitude began to change. I shrugged it off as puberty; after all he was 16 and becoming a man. He was the advocate in the family – my aspiring attorney. His goal from the time he was old enough to understand what lawyers did was to become one himself. He was a straight A student, very respectful, courteous and always mediating a situation between his siblings and friends. He came home from school one day, stating that he was given a position at the school as a student mediator to help resolve issues between classmates – the position was recommended to the Principal by one of his teachers.

I was so proud of him and thankful for him. Despite all my past ill treatment, he was turning out to be an extraordinary young man. I know it seems hard to believe, but he had only once in his life did something that was truly troublesome, and that was at the tender age of 5 when he chased his little sister around the house with a pair of scissors and cut off her hair. He was my helper with his younger siblings and I depended on him more than I realized.

When I received the first phone call informing me that he had missed a class, I asked him about it. He stated he was feeling ill and skipped last period to come home. But the phone calls increased; and now it wasn't only last period, but 3rd period and 1st period classes. Then he started not coming home at all for days at a time. When I finally caught him at home, we spoke and he agreed to straighten up his act. The phone calls trickled down. But that would prove to be the calm before the storm.

One day, while spring cleaning the closets of the house for give- away items, I found within my sons' closet a shoe box with my younger son's sneakers in it. This was odd because the younger son never kept the boxes his shoes came in. My first thought was that this pair must not fit any longer; so I took them out of the box. One shoe dropped to the floor, and out of it, a medium-sized bag fell filled with a white substance. I reached down and picked it up and my heart stopped as I realized that the substance could be drugs.

The children were all out playing and so I called a close friend and asked her to come over right away. I didn't let her get in the door good before I shoved the bag in her hand asking desperately,

"What does this look like to you?"

She took it and stood momentarily stunned, and then the conversation began,

"Where did you get this from?"

"Out of my youngest son's gym shoe in the closet."

"Nooooo, he's not……Noooooooo."

"I don't think it's his."

"Then who do you…. Noooooo not"

I cut her off,

"It would explain his behavior lately, skipping classes, staying out late, not coming home for days at a time."

"But you don't know for sure that this is what we think it is, do you?"

"Well, how am I supposed to find out? Take it to the police?"

"NO! Girl you will go to jail, they will take your house, AND put your kids in the system!"

"Then what are we supposed to do?"

"We?"

"Yes WE you are here and you ain't going nowhere!"

"Ok let's find out first if it is what we think it is and then we can go from there."

We had a mutual friend who had been truly delivered from drug addiction. She has a powerful testimony and so we decided to take the bag to her so that she could identify the contents. I know, I know, not the smartest move. What if we had been in an accident or stopped by the police; or even worse, what if bringing her face to face with her past triggered a relapse? We weren't thinking and **no** we didn't think to pray and ask God what to do either. Off to her home we drove from the suburbs of Chicago into the inner city. In her basement, I brought out the bag and she replied in an unusually calm voice,

"Deidra honey where did you get that?"

I told her and she said,

"Hand me the bag baby."

I did. She opened and sniffed it and then reclosed it, and in an even more calm voice than before she asked,

"Sweetie do you know what this is?"

I replied,

"I think it's cocaine. It's cocaine, isn't it!"

"Correct, do you understand exactly how much cocaine is in this bag?"

"No."

"Well let me put it this way, this amount is not for personal consumption and will bring the one caught with it a considerable amount of time. Your son is in trouble honey he is a runner. They will be looking for a considerable amount of cash to be returned to them for a stash of this quantity. What do you plan to do?"

My heart stopped, the air in the room got extremely thick, the room seemed to be spinning and I heard myself say,

"I'm gonna pass out."

"Honey this is no time to be passing out. You NEED a plan and you need it NOW!"

Without thinking, I took the bag and told my friend to take me home. Once I got home, I flushed the entire bag down the toilet and I sat up and waited for my son to come home. At around 10 p.m. that evening, he came home. His mind was so preoccupied he didn't even see me sitting on the couch. He went into his room, I heard him fumbling around then I heard frantic remarks exploding in anxiety. I went to the door and asked him while holding up the shoe box,

"Are you looking for this?"

His facial expression became eased as he stood up from the floor of the closet trying to figure out how to explain it to me. I stopped him before he could utter one word.

"I flushed it. How could you bring that into my house with your brother and sisters? I could have lost my house! DCFS could have taken ALL OF YOU out of my custody! How could you? WHAT ARE YOU THINKING?!"

I do not believe he heard anything after I said I flushed it, I watched the blood literally drain from his face as he sat back down on the floor.

"You flushed it? Do you know what you just did to me? You FLUSHED IT! WHY WOULD YOU DO THAT! IT DIDN'T BELONG TO ME! OH MY GOD WHAT AM I GOING TO DO NOW! I can't believe that you flushed it...you flushed it?"

I watched the spirit of fear consume his body.

"SON WHO ARE THESE PEOPLE? YOU SEND THEM TO ME I WILL TELL THEM WHAT I DID AND I WILL HANDLE IT."

"Send them to you? ARE YOU CRAZY? MOM THIS IS NOT T.V.! You FLUSHED THEIR MERCHANDISE! WHAT DO YOU THINK THEY ARE GOING TO DO SIT DOWN AND HAVE BIBLE STUDY WITH YOU?! I GOTTA GET OUT OF HERE! They only know the high school I attend; they don't know where I live. I never brought them to your house, or even this neighborhood. I GOTTA GET OUT OF HERE!"

My son ran away from home that night. I sat with the guilt that my son had chosen to sell drugs in an attempt to make money to get away from my home. He didn't want to be there when my husband came back. I got a call a week later from his father who told me that he was with him in Minnesota. The exodus had begun, one down three to go. My youngest son poured out his anger on me. In his mind, I caused his brother to leave him.

He, at 15, was already taller and much bigger than I was. He towered over me and his sisters, his size succeeding in transforming the once very protective presence into a volatile one. I caught him calling one of his sisters a female dog; and when I corrected him, out of sheer defiance, he called her it again, to which my reaction was to slap him for his blatant disrespect. He, in response to the slap, tackled me, causing my head to bounce off the bathroom floor and knocking me unconscious. When I came home from the E.R. with a slight concussion, he apologized profusely for 2 weeks. At the end of the second week, my husband came home.

……. *A time to get and a time to lose, a time to keep and a time to cast away,*

Little by little things started to come up missing in the house. My children's bikes disappeared one by one. I would park my car on a full tank after work, and when I got up in the morning, it would be on empty with a horrible scent inside. Church members started to tell me that they had seen my car and its prominently displayed church bumper-sticker in places that were known for not-so-honorable intentions. Finally, the checks started bouncing, bills began to go unpaid.

How did I handle it? By diving head-first into every church activity offered. My children saw less and less of me as I busied myself with more and more work. I dreaded going home after work and so I made bee-lines to the church instead. Sometimes I involved my children; most often I did not. I left them to defend themselves against whatever attitude greeted them after school.

Finally, after another incident involving my son and one of his sisters, I requested for him to leave my house. (*him I could put out, it hadn't dawned on me to ask the same of my husband*) My son of course went on to oblige my demand, but I wanted my keys first. He was not going to disrespect me and have open access into my house. He refused to give them to me.

The keys were on a plastic chain clipped to his belt loop, and I in the heat of the moment, ordered my youngest daughter to bring me a knife so that I could cut the keys off his pants. Just as I went to slice the plastic key chain, he reached out to block me and I instead succeeded in slicing the palm of his hand. He then grabbed his hand and ran out of the house to a neighbor's, enraged because I had demanded for him to leave and not my husband. He called the police and told them that I had cut him with a knife.

The police came and I was arrested for battery with a deadly weapon against a minor, and child endangerment. I sat in a Cook County Jail cell for 3 days until I saw a judge and the charges were dismissed. After returning home, the environment was hostile to say the least. Unknown to me, my son called his father in Minnesota; and one day while I was at work and my husband was out and about, he met up with his father and went to live with him. It was my oldest daughter who gave me the somber message when I walked in from work and asked her where her brother was. She simply said, *"He's gone. He went to live with his father too."* And then there were two.

My oldest daughter who was 14 began to complain of stomach pain, and because I was the only one employed at the time, my husband had to take her to the doctor. He informed me of my impending status change (that of soon-to-be grandmother) in the only way he knew how; with a sideways comment that he connected to a journal that I had recently found of hers and was keeping to ask her about. The following year, because of stress, I lost my employment. The house went into foreclosure and my car was repossessed. Had I consulted Holy Spirit about allowing him back home? No, of course not. The scripture below explains the reason I had not.

> *"But how are people to call upon Him Whom they have not believed [in Whom they have no faith, on Whom they have no reliance]?"*
> *Romans 10:14a (Amp)*

Right now, you are probably saying, "Wait a minute, I thought you were a believer?" To that, I say I am. You may be asking, "Then why the scripture above?" Because at that time, I believed in God as God the one who created the world and had power over demons. You know, the One who could do great big things. I did not believe in Him as a Father whom I could trust to lead me in my marriage, or with the raising of my children, or with anything else of major importance in my life. God to me was a far- away entity that dealt with universal things, I was responsible for the details of my life.

In chapter two, I showed you all of ways that God had used my former pastor to show me a godly example of fatherhood, of which he did superbly; but at the time, I did not or could not receive the revelation of that. And so after moving to Chicago, God was continuing his process of re-newing my mind in this area; but because I either wouldn't or couldn't see Him as a Father to believe in, have faith in and to rely on, I suffered many dark days.

I believe that because of the incorrect state of my mind, that even if I had gone to the Holy Spirit for guidance about whether or not to allow my husband back in, and He had told me a fraction of what would happen, I wouldn't have believed Him. Why not?

The answer in its simplest form is because I wanted to be married. I *needed* to be married. As long as I was married, it meant that I hadn't failed. I chose to believe that because my husband had called me, God had answered the prayers already sent up.

Before my husband had left, we were in an insect-infested apartment. I looked at my new circumstances and I figured: we are in a house, now the stress of slum lord dwellings is gone. I had a job as an administrative assistant with good benefits. I imagined that there now wouldn't be any stress about money. I had a car and we no longer had to depend on public transportation – even more stress that had been eliminated. I presumed within my own understanding that he now had absolutely no reason to turn to drugs, we had nothing to argue or fight about, God had blessed and all things were fixed. Why not let him back in?

"There is a way that seems right to a man, But its end is the way of death." Proverbs 16:25 (NKJV)

Instead of being happy for all that God had blessed us with, often I was accused by him of thinking that I was better than he was. We argued all the time over everything. Even happy occasions were turned sour. When I received raises at work, I was charged with looking down on him because I made more money than he did. He would remind me that I was nothing, and never would be anything without him. The stress had my weight on a roller-coaster, which succeeded in supplying him with more ammunition to use against my self-esteem.

During all of this, the enemy attacked my mind with all sorts of lies about how God was punishing me because of things in my past – things not done as asked – and the ever-growing resentment that I harbored against my husband.

Later, during a visit with his brother in our then new apartment, I learned that he was living as if single while in Waterloo. Tales of his escapades, he boastfully shared with his brother, as if I were not sitting in the room. His brother spoke up on my behalf which angered him, and he resentfully changed the subject.

Why didn't I speak up? Truthfully, I don't know why. Maybe I was finally beaten down to the point that I could no longer fight back. My youngest daughter must have sensed this because she took matters into her own hands and decided to place Lysol into the container of orange juice that belonged solely to my husband. This act caused him to contact the police and my 12-year-old was taken from my home and placed into foster care for 2 years. My oldest daughter then called her father who also lived in Minnesota, and she and my grandson moved away. I was now alone with a man that I had come to resent intensely.

During all of this, God in His infinite wisdom, via several dreams, called me to preach His wonderful Gospel, after literally running from everyone in leadership that may have gotten any inclination of the call on my life for an *entire year*. Because, let's face it, my life was in ruins, and there had to be some sort of mistake; God sent one of the Elders of the ministry to confront me.

With a single question I was outed, *"Weren't you supposed to come and see us some time ago about the call on your life?"*

My immediate thought was, *"God, You told on me?"* The cat was out of the bag, and I, with fear and trembling, submitted to the interview before the Elder's Council and the subsequent training. I fought through the humiliation of drug-induced spousal abuse, my teenage son fleeing for his life after attempting to sell drugs, being placed in jail, one of my teenage daughter's becoming pregnant, and one of my children being taken from my custody to the end of ministerial training and became licensed – all because of four little words the Holy Spirit had placed in my ear, *"It's not about you."*

Earlier in the year I had been involved in an accident where an 18 wheeler and two cars hit and totaled my car. I now had severe physical pain on top of all of the emotional pain. It was at this time that I made a desperate decision, that of suicide.

As with most people who take their own lives I falsely assumed that things were never going to change. The worse had happened in my eyes. The courts had taken away my youngest child; my oldest had to leave to spare his life, my second oldest son and oldest daughter both left because they couldn't take the atmosphere of our home any longer. I was in a lot of physical pain. My husband preferred drugs to a relationship with me, and all of my praying was falling on what I assumed to be deaf ears because I as a daughter obviously didn't matter to God.

On the day that I had decided that life was no longer worth the sadness and pain, I went to work as usual. On a lunch break, I went to the bank and withdrew enough money to pay for the motel room that I had booked online. At the end of the work day, I cleared my desk as always, but this time, I also removed my pictures – leaving nothing but an envelope addressed to my supervisor containing my letter of resignation. Previous thoughts on this dark journey within another of my books did not lend me these details, but they are streaming in with great clarity as I put pen to paper today. However, I still don't remember ever packing the pills that morning before work. I drove myself to a motel, in the room I took out every pill bottle that my medicine cabinet held. I lined them up and looked at them for hours. In the background, the television was on, and a preacher came on speaking about hope. I muted the television.

"Because of and through the heart of tender mercy and loving-kindness of our God, a Light from on high will dawn upon us and visit [us] To shine upon and give light to those who sit in darkness and in the shadow of death, to direct and guide our feet in a straight line into the way of peace."
Luke 1:78-79 (Amp)

Why didn't I just turn the television off for that matter? Why did I ever turn it on? I don't know, divine intervention maybe. But the television kept summoning my attention; and so I unmuted it and listened. For 24 hours, I cried harder than I had ever cried before. I cried until my tears ran out and my throat was sore. I literally cried myself into a deep sleep. I awoke to the sound of knocking. It was housekeeping telling me that it was time to check out. I left that motel and drove straight to the church, where my friends had been praying and searching for me. One of them took one look at me and said,

"To the prayer room, take her to the prayer room."

There in that prayer room, they labored in love, in warfare and in deliverance. When I left that prayer room, my hope had been restored, and I sought the Lord on behalf of my youngest daughter. At the end of the most heart-wrenching 2 years a mother could ever go through dealing with the Department of Children and Family Services, the judge awarded me custody again of my youngest daughter. She returned home quiet and stayed out of my husband's company as much as she could. My daughter and I became each other's ally, and with her, I hid as much money as I could. One night after he had become severely agitated with my success in hiding money away from him, an argument ensued that ended with me going to the emergency room with a concussion.

> *"He makes me to lie down in green pastures; He leads me beside the still waters. He restores my soul; He leads me in the paths of righteousness for His name's sake." Psalms 23:2-3 (NKJV)*

A week later, my husband's mother took a trip to Minnesota to visit his twin sister and his other siblings and he asked him if we could go up to see her. Since three of my children had relocated back there, I decided that it would be nice for my daughter and I to see them; and so we took a trip. While there, he took the rental car and some money and disappeared for 3 days. I had a conversation with his mother and his twin sister, then I made a decision: when we returned from Minnesota, I and my daughter would move in with my sister.

> *"But when you do a charitable deed, do not let your left hand know what your right hand is doing," Matthew 6:3(NKJV)*

Back in Chicago, I found him a room for rent. On the day that we were moving out of the apartment, we packed the truck in silence. He rode in the truck with my daughter and I in the same silence. At the boarding house, I parked and asked him to come in with me, I left my daughter in the truck. He was willing because he thought that this was our new place. He stood by as I paid the rent for thirty days. I then handed him the keys, a bus card with a month's worth of rides on it, and gave him my cell phone. I turned towards the manager and told him,

> *"After these first thirty days, the rent will be on my husband."*

I then turned towards my husband and told him,

> *"You have a bus card, a cell phone, and 30 days to find employment or you will be homeless."*

After which I turned and walked out of the building. Earlier, I had instructed my daughter to unload his things on the sidewalk. He came out and saw them, he asked in desperation,

"Where are you going?"

I responded with,

"Do you want help with taking your things into the room?"

He asked me again the same question to which I again responded with my previous question. He took a moment to process the situation and responded with a *"yes"*. My daughter and I helped him take his things into his room. On the way back to the truck, he ran behind me and asked with his eyes filled with tears,

"Dee are you leaving me?"

And with my eyes filled with tears I responded, "*Yes.*" I then got in the truck with my daughter and drove off, leaving him standing there on the sidewalk staring as we turned the corner.

While at my sister's home my oldest daughter and

grandson moved back to Chicago and in with us. After four months, I decided that we should relocate to Florida. The plan was for us to temporarily move in with my father. I could feel all of those old daddy issues bubbling up.

I encouraged myself by remembering how the pastor in Minnesota had welcomed me into his life as a daughter. I told myself you can do this; look, he is allowing you to come, isn't that a start? Since he had already agreed to allow us to stay to keep myself from future disappointment, I made an inner vow not to ask him for anything more. I didn't realize it, but I was reaching for familiar stones to rebuild the wall that God had already taken a jackhammer to tear down.

*"He left Judaea, and departed again into Galilee. And he **must needs go** through Samaria." John 4:2-3 (KJV)*

My self-esteem was shot. My value and self-worth was hanging on by the thinnest of threads. I believed that God was angry with my decision to separate from my husband, my relationship with my children was on rocky ground, and to top it all off, food had become my comforter which caused my weight to reflect my emotional turmoil. I needed a breakthrough and it didn't seem as though it was going to come in Chicago, so in February of 2004 off to Florida we went.

"Departed again into Galilee." I like that Jesus had to go back home. Home representing wherever my *"father's house"* was, and since he had relocated to Florida, my Galilee (aka home) was now in a little town called Graceville. Yes, Graceville. Could this be anymore apropos? I needed to take a trip into grace in order for things to be corrected.

"And he must needs go through Samaria." I need to take you for a brief moment to the school of Samaria in order for this next point to be made. Through Samaria was the shortest distance to get to certain regions of Galilee, but because of **their shared bitter history,** those of Jewish descent would rather take the long route of walking around it than crossing through it. As you have seen from some of the details of my life that I for some time had walked the long route around the root of my problem, and now the time had come and the Lord was pressing upon me the need to go back to my father's house to work through our _shared bitter history_ in order for my breakthrough to come.

I went with three goals in mind, two of which I was conscious of. The first goal was a need for God to do what He could do to mend as much as possible the relationship between my father and I. The second goal was to have God to help me mend the relationship between myself and my daughters, as I hoped against all odds would be the catalyst into the restoration of the relationship between me and my sons. The last goal was a subconscious one, I needed help me to determine if I was going to stay married.

> *"For the word of God is living and powerful, and sharper than any two-edged sword, piercing even to the division of soul and spirit, and of joints and marrow, and is a discerner of the thoughts and intents of the heart." Hebrews 4:12 (NKJV)*

A DAUGHTER'S CONTEMPLATION

I have shared many dark moments in this chapter. As you read, what deep hurt has the Holy Spirit revealed unto you?

_____

Were you under the belief that you had already been healed from these?

Know this: if they have been shown to you and there is still pain with the memory, you have not been healed. The Holy Spirit within the timing of the Lord God has said that now is the appointed hour for healing to come. Do not fight against it, take a deep breath, you are able to face it; for if you were not, God would not have allowed the memory to come to the forefront at this time.

"To everything there is a season, and a time to every purpose under the heaven: A time to be born, and a time to die; a time to plant, and a time to pluck up that which is planted; A time to kill, and a time to heal; a time to break down, and a time to build up;" Eccl. 3:1-3 (KJV)

Pray with me,

"Father You are all knowing, and merciful. Your word has said that in You I may have perfect peace in spite of the tribulation and trials and distress and frustration that I will encounter in this world. You have told me to be of good cheer, to take courage be confident in the fact that You have overcome the world. LORD GOD I trust You! I believe that You have done exactly what Your word says. In Your word I am told that healing is in your wings, that deliverance is the children's bread and that you will make my enemies to sit at the table while you BLESS ME. In these promises I now stand and willingly allow you to enter into this dark place within my heart and place your light. Heal me, make me new, create within me a clean heart and renew within me a right spirit. I renounce the ties of the enemy in this situation and I allow you to pluck up that which has been planted by the enemy of my soul to interfere with the relationship that a daughter was meant to have with her father. I surrender this piece of my heart into your hands to cleanse with hyssop so that I then can give it unto You without reservation and without fear. In Jesus name I pray as you begin the process of making me a new creation in You."

CHAPTER FOUR

Assurance Policy

Daughters, I feel the very real need to put in the middle of this journey a practical step to rearing up children without the damaging emotional walls of low or no self-worth. Those of you who are in the unfortunate situations of being single mothers, because the fathers are unable to be in the lives of their children due to duty of country, sickness, death, or are unwilling because they are themselves walking within the generational curses passed down to them by non-present fathers. Think of these steps as, *"Assurance Policies,"* For they will assure one in their identity in God and build up their self-esteem in a manner that will not be haughty or arrogant but firmly established.

Deuteronomy 6:2-7 says,

Step 1.

*"That thou mightest **fear** the Lord thy God, **to keep all** his statutes and his commandments, which I command*

thee, thou, and thy son, and thy son's son, all the days of thy life; and that thy days may be prolonged."

Mother, you are going to need all the help that you can get in raising your children. What better place to gain this help than from He who created the both of you? God knows everything that you will need to get them where they need to be, but first you must be firmly rooted so that you can show them the way.

Step 2.

*"**Hear therefore**, O Israel, **and observe to do it**; that it may be well with thee, and that ye may increase mightily, as the Lord God of thy fathers hath promised thee, in the land that floweth with milk and honey."*

God speaks, and when He does, He expects us to listen. He not only expects us to listen, but He expects us to do what He has instructed. Go to Him in prayer and ask Him how to do the assignment of motherhood. He will lead you if you seek Him for instructions.

Step 3.

*"Hear, O Israel: The Lord our God is one Lord: And **thou shalt love** the Lord thy God **with all thine** heart, and*

with all *thy soul, and **with all** thy might. And these words, which I command thee this day, shall be in thine heart: And **thou shalt teach** them diligently unto thy children, and **shalt talk** of them when thou sittest in thine house, and when thou walkest by the way, and when thou liest down, and when thou risest up."*

Mothers, in order for you to give the love to your children that they will need, you will need to know the love of and for the Father. This love must consume your whole heart and soul, and then you have to teach this love to your children by showing them who they are in God through the example of Jesus.

Teach them that:

"Children are a gift from the Lord; they are a reward from him." Psalm 127:3 (NLT)

"And the very hairs on your head are all numbered. So don't be afraid; you are more valuable to God than a whole flock of sparrows." Luke 12:7(NLT)

and that they should continually be-

"turning your ear to wisdom and applying your heart to understanding—indeed, if you call out for insight and

cry aloud for understanding, and if you look for it as for silver and search for it as for hidden treasure, then you will understand the fear of the Lord and find the knowledge of God. For the Lord gives wisdom; from his mouth come knowledge and understanding." Proverbs 2:2-6 (NIV)

"Lean on, trust in, and be confident in the Lord with all your heart and mind and do not rely on your own insight or understanding." Proverbs 3:5 (AMP)

and that as parents we are told by Jesus to-

"Allow the children to come to Me—do not forbid or prevent or hinder them—for to such belongs the kingdom of God." Mark 10:14b (AMP)

and that God the Father says this about them-

"For I know the plans I have for you," declares the Lord, "plans to prosper you and not to harm you, plans to give you hope and a future." Jeremiah 29:11 (NIV)

"God said, Let Us [Father, Son, and Holy Spirit] make mankind in Our image, after Our likeness, ... So God created man in His own image; in the image of God He created him; male and female He created them." Genesis 1:26a,27(AMP)

If my mother would have been able to teach me this before she fell into deep depression, before the dissolution of her marriage, and before my father moved out, I believe that I would have walked a different path. I would have also been able to teach this to my own children and cut out all the unfortunate suffering that they went through at my hands and because of my choices.

My hope is that the future generations of my bloodline will know this, and that both your present and future generations will too.

LIFE APPLICATION

Ask your daughter(s) what they really think of themselves.

Show them the scriptures listed and find others that will dispel wrong images.

Have an honest conversation about your own self-image and share what God has done to correct the wrong ideas you yourself held.

Although this book is primarily geared toward daughters, this chapter is for sons as well.

The past is the past. If you have not been practicing the suggestions listed in this chapter, begin today; it's not too late.

CHAPTER FIVE

Recovery of Worth

"And when the Pharisees saw this, they said to His disciples, 'Why does your Master eat with tax collectors and those [preeminently] sinful?' But when Jesus heard it, He replied, 'Those who are strong and well (healthy) have no need of a physician, but those who are weak and sick.'"
Matthew 9:11-12

This chapter will be a challenging one. Within it, I will reveal some hard truths that I hope will cause you to face some of your own in order for the recovery to begin. Some of those truths will be taking a look into what others have done to contribute to my past state, and while reading, some of your lived trespasses may surface to reveal the present state you are in, but the majority of the reflection will be on *Me* – which means that your reflections are going to come for the sole purpose of exposing to you, *You*... **_Daughter_** it is vital for you to see what you are doing to continue to propel the bondages of low self-worth or low self-esteem; the two terms are interchangeable.

There are basic stages that one will go through as God transforms His daughter into the individual that He created her to be. The first of course is **_Acknowledgment_** of the deficiency.

"Let us search out and examine our ways, and turn back to the Lord;" Lam.3:40 (NKJV)

Are you allowing ungodly practices and people to rule your day to day life?

Do you allow others to speak to you or treat you in an offensive manner?

Is your speech laced with hopelessness and lack of respect for both others and yourself?

How about your attitude, is it negative and insecure?

Do you have a poor self-image of yourself?

Do you act out in ways that are harmful to you and others?

Within your day to day living are you angry, un-submissive, argumentative, and generally unhappy?

Do you find that people are anxious to get away from your presence?

Do you believe that your way of thinking is the only correct way of thinking?

Do you have a hard time forgiving people for the wrong committed?

Are you unteachable?

Self-examination is often prompted by others because it is always easier to see what is going on within someone else. The Father has a little something to say about that if this is always your practice;

"And why do you look at the speck in your brother's eye, but do not consider the plank in your own eye? Or how can you say to your brother, 'Let me remove the speck from your eye'; and look, a plank is in your own eye? Hypocrite! First remove the plank from your own eye, and then you will see clearly to remove the speck from your

brother's eye." Matthew 7:3-5(NKJV)

However, when we are used by God to point out some of the above behaviors in someone else, we are instructed by God to do so,

"in humility correcting those who are in opposition, if God perhaps will grant them repentance, so that they may know the truth,"2Tim.2:25 (NKJV)

In my father's house, the atmosphere was a bit tense. He had not spoken to wife number three about my upcoming arrival. She was genuinely shocked when I entered her home with two daughters and a grandson, and after taking one look at our entire luggage ensemble, it became embarrassingly apparent that our presence was going to be longer than a mere visit. Needless to say, for her, this our first meeting encounter became instantly unpleasant. I however, found myself enjoying the idea that this time he chose me over a wife.

Did you see that? The unseemly, un-Christian behavior displayed by *Me*. It is not loving or peaceful to enjoy the discomfort of others. I do not know why my father chose not to inform his wife of our discussions, but as she pointed out within a private conversation between she and I; the hospitable thing for me to do would have been to ask to speak to her during at least one of those conversations seeing that it is also her home too.

Special note here, ***<u>You cannot find worth within the devaluing of another's</u>***.   This train of thinking is of the enemy and will render counterfeit self-esteem because it comes at the hand of taking away someone else's.

That split second moment of joy over the thought that "*he chose me over her*" is all that was needed by the enemy to create an atmosphere of tension and strife. In me rose pride, and for two days I walked around her house as if she were the visitor. Yes, I made her anxious to be out of my presence because I was oozing haughtiness. I was making this new wife pay for the sins of the previous one. So let's see that would be transference, which was solely connected to unforgiveness. Within this paragraph, I have highlighted two behaviors from the acknowledgement list above that I was guilty of.

After two days, she had reached her limit and requested a side bar conversation between just the two of us. Once the air between us was clear, a slightly more inviting atmosphere began to arrive.

> *"Now therefore thus says the Lord of hosts: Consider your ways and set your mind on what has come to you. You have sown much, but you have reaped little; you eat, but you do not have enough; you drink, but you do not have your fill; you clothe yourselves, but no one is warm; and he who earns wages has earned them to put them in a bag with holes in it. Thus says the Lord of hosts: Consider your ways (your previous and present conduct) and how you have fared." Haggai 1:5-7 (Amp)*

Before we move forward, I want you to revisit the questions within the *"Acknowledgement"* stage. OK, now that those questions are in the forefront of your mind, we can move on to the second stage of recovery which is **_Connection._**

The above scripture tells us to consider the way we have been living and to look at what our outcome has been. Within my sanctified imagination, I have chosen to break the scripture into parts that will highlight the different areas of our lives.

"You have sown much, but you have reaped little"

Emotionally – the one battling with low self-esteem will make themselves a dependent follower, always giving of themselves in hopes of receiving attention, which is incorrectly translated as love. The problem that occurs is that they always seem to attach themselves to the individual that is a taker. Once the taker sees the emotionally dependent trait in the giver, the taker will then by automatic default begin to give only the minimum and sometimes even less than that. The taker knows that the giver gives out of a fear of losing. The giver will give, give, give and the taker will receive, receive, receive without really reciprocating a thing, causing the giver to reap little.

In chapter three I revealed some of my dependent behavior; I carried this trait not only within my marriage but in other relationships as well. I would give all of me (well, what I thought was all of me) and in return I found myself lacking, love, attention, care, and respect. Why? Because the takers in my life realized that my giving was out of fear of being alone and somehow this diminished their responsibility to give true love, attention and respect. They saw an opportunity to live as they wanted because I was always going to be there no matter what.

"you eat, but you do not have enough; you drink, but you do not have your fill."

Physically- Often those who suffer with low self-worth also suffer with poor body images. They perceive that the cause of their diminished value is due to the fact that they are too thin, too fat, too tall, too short, too etc. The emotional eater re-enacts the above verse every time food is used as a comforter instead of the fuel God intended it to be for the body. This verse is not only speaking of physical eating but mental and emotional eating as well.

How does one eat emotionally? One example is by parading people in their lives on an intimate level by engaging in many sexual relationships but never really connecting emotionally. This is one of things I personally did in an attempt to show myself that I was desirable. In my reasoning the more men that I was able to attract, the more my worth was increased. In actuality I was causing more damage rather than building my self-worth.

Mentally one eats with thoughts that tell them I need to take this and this and have that too, always plotting their next conquest. Within this mindset the belief is that the acquisition of material things will build up their self-worth. As I write a scene from *"Pretty Woman"* comes to mind. It is the one where Richard Gere states that the very first company that he took over and sold off piece by piece was his father's. He thought that taking something that his father valued would compensate for the lack of worth he felt from his father. But as I stated in the beginning of this chapter, ***You cannot find worth within the devaluing of another's.***

As the movie progressed we learned that he had become very wealthy taking things in this manner, but his appetite for worth was yet unfulfilled. He had spent his life plotting takeovers one conquest at a time and still he found himself in the psychiatrist office paying $10,000 to find out that the root of his compulsion was anger. He had drunk the milk of success yet he still was not filled. Looking at this movie from a spiritual standpoint Richard Gere's character was suffering from low self-esteem brought on by abandonment and rejection.

Abandonment and Rejection are the same two spirits that sabotaged my self- esteem and caused a lot of deep hurt. I felt rejected when my father refused to buy the more expensive necklace and pay for the driving course. I felt abandoned by him as I, along with my sisters, suffered the various verbal, physical, and emotional abuses at the hand of his second wife; and when he turned to me that day and asked where I wanted to live after her ultimatum, abandonment and rejection opened wide the door for low self-esteem and others to step right in and reside along with them.

In Florida, it was my father whom initiated the conversation that would ignite change in my heart towards him. Previously, I had admitted that I had struggled with forgiving him for ten years and although I had finally allowed God to help me forgive him, we were still quite alienated from one another.

Sitting in the living room of his home I was able to express my true feelings and tell him about the abuse suffered at the hands of his second wife that had been the catalyst that led to our altercation that day. I was surprised to learn that my presumptions all of those years had in fact been wrong. He declared that he had no idea that she had done any of the things that she had, because she was careful not to do them in his presence.

He sat silently for a moment and then asked why I hadn't spoken up then. I told him I did to one of his older sisters, thinking that she would in turn tell him. He stated that she never did. He then asked why I hadn't told him myself, and I at that time had no answer. I didn't know then that I felt I had no right to.

"you clothe yourselves, but no one is warm;"

Intellectually-I am not going to use the usual definitions of 'clothe' and 'warm.' I want to go deeper. Clothe: "endow with a particular quality." Warm: "having, showing, or expressive of enthusiasm, affection, or kindness." Just by replacing the words clothe and warm with their definitions we see the following;

"You endow with a particular quality yourselves, but no one has or shows expressive enthusiasm, affection or kindness."

Low self-worth causes the individual to put on a mask to cover up their feelings of inadequacy. A life of pretense is lived as they clothe themselves with their desired idea of particular qualities so that they may seem on the outside as everyone else, but on the inside there is no enthusiasm, no real affection, nor kindness especially towards themselves or for others.

"and he who earns wages has earned them to put them in a bag with holes in it."

Financially- How is one that suffers from low self-esteem affected financially? I want to point back to the movie "Pretty Woman." Richard Gere's character was extremely wealthy and yet he was also extremely joyless. In spite of all of his money, he still had a human sized void in his life. He made money and saw something that he thought would bring him joy, but after attaining it he would remain joyless. He basically put his money into a bag with holes in it. Money doesn't fix low self-esteem it just allows you the ability to do a lot more damage as you throw money at a problem that is spiritual in nature.

On the flip side, one can be affected financially because low self-esteem has caused them to live life as an underachiever, who was unmotivated and lacked self-confidence. Such an individual would miss out on wealth-building opportunities for fear of failure, and in some cases, fear of success, not believing enough in their ability to maintain what was needed to sustain the success achieved.

Lack of self-confidence in my ability as a writer stopped me for 15 years from following my passion. I've told this story before, but it bears telling again. When I was 26 years of age, and on the encouragement of my best friend, I wrote my first play. We needed a fundraiser for a local food pantry and because she had read something I had written in letter form, she told everyone that I already written a play.

Her insistence that my love letter was a play inspired me to turn it into one, with six scenes and 15 characters. We rehearsed for four months, got radio advertisement, and on the night before our grand debut, my children and I built a set out of cardboard boxes and other furniture that was in the church at the time. The show was a hit! Accolades came from everyone; one church member in particular gave hers with an apology.

She started her comments with a confession,

"I owe you an apology."

Why? She said that she had persuaded someone not to come to the show because in her words,

"It was written by one of our young adults and probably won't be very good."

Why do I remember those words verbatim? Because those words were used by the enemy to literally arrest my future, my finances, and my self-confidence for 15 years.

After accepting her praise and her apology, a woman that I had never seen before stepped up to me and asked if I was the writer? To which I responded yes. She then went on to ask if I had ever thought about writing professionally. I replied no, to which she replied,

"Well when you do give me a call," as she handed me her business card. She was a talent agent who heard the advertisement on the radio and decided to take a gamble.

I never called her. Why? Because I had also accepted with the praise and apology as another severe blow to my self-esteem and the fear of failure joined the spirits of rejection, abandonment, and low self-worth. I heard over and over,

"If she, someone who knows me thinks that my work wouldn't be any good what will people who don't know me think?"

Logically, the answer to that fear-evoking question was in the palm of my hand in the form of a business card, but I allowed fear to override logic. I tucked my passion for writing away not to put pen to paper again until 15 years later. Ironically, it was at the request of church members in my new church who were seeking someone to write a skit.

"If you decide that it's a bad thing to worship God, then choose a god you'd rather serve—and do it today. Choose one of the gods your ancestors worshiped from the country beyond The River, or one of the gods of the Amorites, on whose land you're now living. As for me and my family, we'll worship God." Joshua 24: 15 (Message)

Decide. Daughter, the next stage in your recovery must come in the form of a decision. After acknowledging that there is an issue with your self-esteem and connecting your past or current behavior with the root of the issue, it is time for you to make a decision. Will you remain as you are or will you trust and allow the One who created you to resolve the issue once and for all? Joshua made it plain in the scripture above. With all of the intellectual ideals, and vast array of choice that is before you, you must come to a place of decision for yourself, as much as He wants you to succeed, God is not going to make the decision for you He gave you a free will.

I personally believe that because you are reading this book you have made a decision to become free from the weights that so easily beset you. Will it be hard? Sometimes. But you are well able to weather the storm. Just look at what you've already overcome. The end result far outweighs the struggle of getting to the place of total freedom.

> *"Therefore submit to God. Resist the devil and he will flee from you." James 4:7 (NKJV)*

The above scripture is not only talking about resisting sinful behaviors but it says to resist the devil period. Any words that stunt your growth and distort your image; any act rendered against you that is devised to beat you down into abusive submission are words and acts sent from Satan the devil, the enemy of your soul, mind and your body. We are instructed to RESIST the devil. Every spirit that brings destruction, chaos, misery and death is of the devil. Low self-esteem, rejection, abandonment, fear in all its forms are evil spirits of the devil and we are instructed to RESIST the devil and he will flee.

One way to resist is to **<u>Renounce:</u>** *"To formally declare one's abandonment of (a claim, right, or possession). To refuse to recognize or abide by any longer. To proclaim that one will no longer engage in or support."*

Daughter, it is time for you to formally declare your abandonment and possession of low self-worth! It is time to refuse to recognize or abide by any longer the rulings of low self-esteem. Proclaim that you will no longer engage in or support lack of self-confidence, poor body images, co-dependent relationships, insecurity, fear or anything else associated with the further dismantling of your value.

Renouncing is the falling out of agreement with the lies and schemes of the enemy within your life and is stage four of the plan of recovery of your worth. The Word of God teaches us to,

"Be well balanced (temperate, sober of mind), be vigilant and cautious at all times; for that enemy of yours, the devil, roams around like a lion roaring [[a]in fierce hunger], seeking someone to seize upon and devour." 1 Peter 5:8(Amp)

Daughter, as the Lord reveals the areas that the enemy has creeped in and wreaked havoc within your life renounce them. As you renounce, command the enemy to leave your mind, body, and emotions; as they are expelled, you must then fill your heart and mind with the Word of God which will allow you to live your life guided by the fruits of the Holy Spirit. The Holy Spirit empowers you to become well balanced, vigilant and cautious so that at all times you become aware of the schemes of the devil against you.

During those two months in my father's home, the relationship between he and I began to mend. The gulf that was once between us grew smaller and smaller. We were even able to laugh about some of the things he suffered with wife number two after I had moved out. He told me that he was sorry for all that I had gone through, and for his lack of observation during those years. Whenever a friend would come by the house he would proudly introduce me as the only daughter that had chosen to come and live near dear old dad. I felt my heart opening and my acceptance of him as a father becoming restored.

> *"for that enemy of yours, the devil, roams around like a lion roaring [[a]in fierce hunger], seeking someone to seize upon and devour."*

Everyone was pleased but the enemy, and so he tried one more fail ditch effort to distort my view of fatherhood. I had begun to heal. My faith in my position as a daughter was beginning its re-alignment.

I want to place a special note here; the process differs from person to person. In some, restoration and healing is immediate, the daughter quickly sees herself as God intends, as a well-loved daughter of both her earthly and heavenly fathers and her relationship grows instantly with the LORD in leaps and bounds.

For others the process is a little slower. Depending on the level of hurt experienced and the **<u>hardness of the heart of the daughter,</u>** it may take a little more time for re-alignment to occur, other lessons may have to be learned first, there may be deeper healing that needs to happen. Don't compare your process to anyone else's. God knows where you are, and He knows exactly how to get you to where you need to be, when you need to be there.

Alright, as I was saying, my faith in my position as a daughter was beginning its re-alignment when one night after dinner, my grandson who was 2 years old at the time wandered into the kitchen on his own. My father brought him to the back of the house where my daughters and I were engrossed in a movie. He interrupted us with a stern statement,

> *"You all need to keep an eye on him. I found him in the kitchen."*

My youngest daughter who was 14 grabbed him up while tickling him asked playfully, *"what were you doing in that kitchen boy?"*

His tiny voice replied, *"I want some water."* I then asked her to take him into the kitchen to give him some water. She obeyed, and moments later, I heard my father calling my name. I came into the living room and he asked,

"Why is she in the kitchen?"

Uncertain about the tone in his voice, I said playfully,

"Well sir, the child is fetching some water for the wee one, why didn't you ask her I'm sure she would have told you."

This to my surprise angered him. He immediately jumped up and began to state in a sterner voice than the last,

"THIS IS MY HOUSE! YOU DON'T ASK ME WHY I DON'T DO SOMETHING! I DON'T WANT CHILDREN IN MY KITCHEN! WHATEVER THEY NEED, YOU GET IT FOR THEM!"

I need to stop the story right here for a moment and pull from the list of acknowledgment, behavior question number seven,

> *"Within your day to day living are you angry, **un-submissive**, **argumentative**, and generally unhappy?"*

My response to his command was,

> *"My daughters are 14 and 16 years old they are capable of cooking, cleaning and getting a glass of water. Now, the baby I understand, but I am not going to serve teenagers who are well able to do things for themselves."*

Remember the scripture in 1 Peter, *"Be well balanced (temperate, sober of mind), be vigilant and cautious at all times; for that enemy of yours, the devil, roams around like a lion roaring [[a]in fierce hunger], seeking someone to seize upon and devour."*?

I was not temperate, sober minded, vigilant or cautious. And because of all the things I was not, the enemy was able to seize both my father and I that day. My father responded to my comment with,

> *"YOU DON'T BACK TALK ME IN MY HOUSE! YOU CAN GET YOUR CHILDREN, and YOUR THINGS, AND GET OUT!"*

I have to visit the acknowledgement list again this time for question number nine,

> *"Do **you believe** that your way of thinking is the only correct way of thinking?"*

Which evidently is the reason why I responded with,

> *"I'm not back talking you. What's right is right and you are wrong daddy you're wrong! I will gladly take my children and my things and get out of your home!"*

I turned to walk towards the bedroom, and before I knew what had happened, he had come around the couch and was in the dining room where he slapped me on the side of my head. The force sent me flying off my feet into the kitchen where I hit and slid across the floor. His wife ran into the dining room screaming his name. He was now at the safe trying to open it, inside of it was where he kept his gun. His wife ran over and stood between him and the safe. He then went and picked up the phone and dialed 911. He told them that he had someone in his home that he wanted removed.

The police arrived and took one look at my face and asked me if I wanted to press charges. I told them no. They informed my father that they didn't need my request to arrest him, but they would adhere to my wishes. However, if he placed a hand on me or anyone else in the home, he would be the one removed. I moved out two weeks later. It took him two months to come to my home and apologize for his behavior of which to my surprise I accepted.

That entire incident would not have taken place if I had only said, yes sir. Was my father wrong? Yes, but was it my place at that time to tell him so? No. What caused him to fly up in such a rage? I surmise that there were two causes, the first,

"for that enemy of yours, the devil, roams around like a lion roaring [[a]in fierce hunger], seeking someone to seize upon and devour."

And the second, my lack of honor, the Word of God says,

"Honor your father and your mother, that your days may be long upon the land which the Lord your God is giving you." Exodus 20:12

Notice the scripture doesn't say honor them if you agree with them, or honor them when they have done all that a father should do. It only says to honor them. When

I responded with anything other than 'yes sir', my father took that as disrespectful and his eyes I was not honoring him.

He did not see the then 38-year-old woman standing before him voicing her opinion, he only saw *daughter*; a daughter who was disrespecting him in front of his wife, in his home. And because of that the enemy latched on to his anger and was going to cause him to sin. Had he gotten into that safe like he was trying to my days on this earth would have been cut. For in the heat of passion he would have taken my life.

I should have been vigilant and paid attention to the clues. He was agitated when he brought my grandson back into the room. He was also distressed when he called me to the front, and there was definite tension in that first question of his. Maybe he was in the middle of an argument with his wife, maybe he was in some sort of physical pain, I don't know. But what I do know is that as wrong as the behavior exhibited by my father was, I had a hand in it because of the attitudes adopted by me due to low self-worth. I decided to renounce the voices of the enemy that bombarded me after this incident which allowed me not to remain "unteachable," and stopped me from reverting to past behavior of "unforgiveness."

The final stage that must be entered into is that of **Commitment.**

> *"Roll your works upon the Lord [commit and trust them wholly to Him; He will cause your thoughts to become agreeable to His will, and] so shall your plans be established and succeed."*
> *Proverbs 16:3 (Amp)*

If you want to get to the point that I had gotten to in order to be able to renounce the voices of the enemy, you must become committed first and foremost to the Lord. Once you commit your thoughts to the Lord He will begin to show you errors in your thinking. It took my father two months to apologize, but it also took the Lord two months to work out the ill-formed opinions of my past that were pushing their views onto the incident. I had to stand back from the emotions of the event, and back track over every detail from the moment he had brought my grandson into the room to the time the police arrived.

This was emotionally very hard for me at first. My heart was hurting and all I wanted to do was protect it. The only way I knew how to protect it was to harden it. God had to show me that I couldn't harden my heart against my father without hardening my heart against Him. The second commitment must be made to yourself. You must commit to maintaining the deliverance that is received at each stage that it is received. Sometimes you may require help in obtaining the deliverance that is needed this will involve you overcoming your apprehension about confessing your struggles to others. Seek the Lord's direction of where you can go to receive sound biblical ministry in the area of deliverance.

If your home church does not currently operate within the ministry of deliverance, then seek a ministry that does. I am not saying withdraw from your current ministry, I am saying go where the help can be given, get the deliverance that is needed and if God has not released you from the ministry that you are currently an active member of, go back and tell them about the goodness of God's delivering power. Do you remember when Jesus healed the man in the tombs in chapter 5 of the book of Mark? In the 19th verse Jesus tells the man,

> *"Go home to your own people and tell them how much the Lord has done for you, and how he has had mercy on you."*

The word says that,

> *"They triumphed over him by the blood of the Lamb and by the word of their testimony; they did not love their lives so much as to shrink from death." Rev. 12:11 (NIV)*

In order for the Body of Christ to triumph over the enemy, we need two things according to these scriptures: THE BLOOD and our Testimony. Often, people are stuck in traditional cycles and do not know of the many facets of God's work because it hasn't been done or taught before, but if someone witnesses something that hasn't been seen before and testifies about it, it opens the door for others to be able to personally witness it too. You never know, your daughter may be the one whom God wants to use to bring a deliverance ministry to your current house of worship so become committed in both receiving and testifying of your own deliverance.

After things had been placed on the right road of recovery between my father and I, there was the little matter of my marriage. I had been in Florida for 7 months when my husband and I had a conversation in August of 2004. He relayed to me that he had placed himself within an inpatient rehab facility that had a program that consisted of 3 phases. He informed me that he had been there for 10 months and that his release date was that upcoming October from the 3rd phase of the program.

He asked if I would be willing to give our marriage one more try. He stated that he felt that my family, friends and church members had all become a part of our marriage and if I allowed us to work on it without outside influences we may have a shot at making it.

I prayed and prayed. I wanted my marriage to work. I wanted our family to heal. This time I sat my daughters down and had a conversation with them about his return. I tried to the best of my ability to explain to them the need for me to give him this one more shot. My youngest daughter to my surprise said that she would try, my oldest daughter informed me that she and her son would be moving out upon his arrival.

In September, on a trip back to Chicago to attend the home-going of one the Elders of the church I had been a member of, I scheduled a visit with my husband to view his progress and the program. When I got back to Florida, my husband called me and told me that the counselor did not agree with his decision to relocate to Florida upon his graduation.

When I asked why, he said that he didn't believe he was ready for that type of responsibility yet and that he should strongly consider staying another 6 months. I told him that he should pray about it. The next day I got a call from my husband, he was on the Greyhound bus heading to Florida. My oldest daughter moved out as promised upon his arrival.

My husband in an effort to become as accommodating as he possibly could, visited the church I had become a member of; but didn't feel as though it was the right place for him, and so I agreed to visit other houses of faith until he found the one he felt led to join. At this new place of worship, the pastor helped him to get employment. He then as a good faith jester requested marriage counseling from the pastor and his wife to begin the work on our unity as husband and wife. We started to become active in ministry.

Things looked as if they were going to be alright then one payday he came home and told me he was going to take a ride with one of the church members to cash his check. He returned 3 hours later, but instead of being dropped off in front of the house he had the person to let him out at the corner. He didn't know that I was looking out of the window at the same time of his arrival (because I was wondering what was taking him so long.) I watched him walk across the street and go to the side of the house. Something in the pit of my stomach turned into knots. Instantly, a thought came to me to take the trash out – the can was on the same side of the house where he had disappeared out of my view.

I ran into the kitchen grabbed the trash bag and opened the back door as I walked around to the side of the house, my heart stopped. There, in broad daylight, on the side of the house, was my husband holding a make-shift pipe, smoking cocaine. He stopped in mid-hit, looked me in my eyes and said,

"I just messed up didn't I?"

I responded,

"No you didn't just mess up you've been messing up for quite some time."

I went into the house and cried like I hadn't cried in a long time. It had been over 365 days since he had done drugs. Both of my daughters were gone from the house at this time, he was working, I was working, we were working on our marriage. We had joined the church that he had picked, everything was as he needed it to be, there were no stressful triggers and yet here he was choosing yet again drugs over me. The words of that counselor came flooding back to my mind. *"you're not ready for that type of responsibility yet."*

It would take five more months after that incident for me to come to terms with the reality that my husband was incapable of being married at this time in his life. In a desperate move to force him to choose a life with me over drugs, I requested to move into a smaller unit. I quit my full-time job at the hospital and accepted a part-time position at McDonalds.

I told my husband that he was now responsible for the two major bills of the household, the rent and water bill; if neither got paid we would be evicted. I would be responsible for the electricity and the food. Four months later, we were evicted. With my heart broken and my self-esteem back in the danger zone, I realized that I alone could not want for him what he had not yet become settled within himself to want, and the next day after a Mother's Day sermon entitled, "*When Helping You Is Hurting Me*" I finally made the decision that was needed to get me on the road of further recovery of my self-worth, I and my youngest daughter who had come back home went into a shelter for battered women. It was under the guiding of the counselors at that place I received the help needed to file for a divorce.

In my book "What's Done in This House" I tell about some of the things that I learned in that shelter, but it wasn't until I got out and a year later moved back to Chicago that many other major milestones would begin to manifest on my journey to recovery.

From 2007-2015, I would require healing from two failed engagements and a third relationship that had my heart entangled within a soul tie for six years before I was finally set free. With each unsuccessful encounter I had to become more committed in keeping the dismantling of the rebuilding of my self-esteem from occurring. I did it by becoming transparent. I told whatever I needed to tell including the embarrassing things that, quote- leaders are not supposed to struggle with- unquote in order to keep the enemy from taking control of my emotions and mind.

A final special note here, leaders are simply men and women who have the same struggles as everyone else, our ability to lead comes from the LORD and His grace that gives us our ability to rise above those struggles when they come, even and especially after we have fallen prey to some. *"For a righteous man may fall seven times. And rise again, But the wicked shall fall by calamity." Proverbs 24:16 (NKJV)*

"Open up before God, keep nothing back; he'll do whatever needs to be done: He'll validate your life in the clear light of day." Psalms 37:5 (Message)

Today, I can truthfully say that I know that I have value. And it is not found in my hairstyle, my dress size, my bank account, or my marital status. My value is found within the ONE who created me in HIS IMAGE, *"So God created man in His own image; in the image of God He created him; male and female He created them." Genesis 1:27 (NKJV)*

Every hair on my head is divinely numbered. The shape of my face, eyes, and nose, lips, legs, thighs, hips, and toes were hand crafted by the ULTIMATE POTTER. The color of my hair, eyes and skin was PERFECTLY blended according to his DIRECT specifications. My height and the build of my frame were EXQUISITELY selected just for me. When The Father was done creating my mold He was delighted and said in pitch harmony with Jesus and the Holy Spirit BEAUTIFULLY, and WONDERFULLY fashioned is She! We shall endow her with gifts and talents that will bring joy to many. She shall proclaim Our power from the rooftops! Strength and Perseverance shall be in her DNA. Creativity shall flow from her like a stream, and the LOVE of US shall draw many to US. My FATHER looked at me, *"And God saw everything that He had made, and behold, it was very good (suitable, pleasant) and **He approved it completely….**" Genesis 1:31(Amp)*

And guess what DAUGHTER, THE SAME GOES FOR <u>YOU!</u>

…. And our worth is far above rubies.

OBSERVATIONS

What behaviors from the list within the Acknowledgement stage are you exhibiting or have exhibited?

Are you willing to admit them to someone that can help you become accountable for your behavior?

What connections were made for you as you read the chapter?

Has the Holy Spirit revealed any mindsets that you believed that are wrong, and are you willing to have your mind renewed in those areas?

What decisions have you made regarding the restoration of your self-worth?

As the Holy Spirit reveals erred beliefs, and spiritual strongholds within your life, are you ready to renounce your agreement with them so that the healing can begin?

What commitments will you have to make in order to become healed and to maintain your deliverance where your self-esteem is concerned?

Also Available From Faith Walk Publishing

Deidra Saddler

What's Done In This HOUSE

HEALING & DELIVERANCE FROM ABUSE

DEIDRA SADDLER

www.ingramcontent.com/pod-product-compliance
Lightning Source LLC
Chambersburg PA
CBHW021131300426
44113CB00006B/381